LIFE'S LITTLE BOOK OF
WISDOM FOR
Students

Quotations by Karen Moore are taken from *God's Graduate: Continuing Education for Everyday Life*, published by Barbour Publishing, Inc.

Scripture quotations marked KJV are taken from the King James Version of the Bible.

Scripture quotations marked MSG are from *THE MESSAGE*. Copyright © by Eugene H. Peterson 1993, 1994, 1995, 1996, 2000, 2001, 2002. Used by permission of NavPress Publishing Group.

Scripture quotations marked NIV are taken from the HOLY BIBLE, NEW INTERNATIONAL VERSION®. NIV®. Copyright © 1973, 1978, 1984 by International Bible Society. Used by permission of Zondervan. All rights reserved.

Scripture quotations marked NKJV are taken from the New King James Version®. Copyright © 1982 by Thomas Nelson, Inc. Used by permission. All rights reserved.

Scripture quotations marked TLB are taken from The Living Bible copyright © 1971. Used by permission of Tyndale House Publishers, Inc., Wheaton, Illinois 60189. All rights reserved.

Cover image © Michael Prince/CORBIS

Published by Barbour Publishing, Inc., P.O. Box 719, Uhrichsville, Ohio 44683, www.barbourbooks.com

Our mission is to publish and distribute inspirational products offering exceptional value and biblical encouragement to the masses.

Printed in China.

LIFE'S LITTLE BOOK OF WISDOM FOR
Students

BARBOUR
PUBLISHING

THERE WILL COME A TIME WHEN
YOU THINK EVERYTHING IS FINISHED.
THAT WILL BE THE BEGINNING.

LOUIS L'AMOUR

MOST PEOPLE ARE ABOUT AS HAPPY
AS THEY MAKE UP THEIR MINDS TO BE.

ABRAHAM LINCOLN

Who stops being better stops being good.

OLIVER CROMWELL

DO NOT WAIT FOR EXTRAORDINARY
SITUATIONS TO DO GOOD;
TRY TO USE ORDINARY SITUATIONS.

JEAN PAUL RICHTER

A wise man will make more opportunities than he finds.

FRANCIS BACON

If you take too long in deciding
what to do with your life,
you'll find you've done it.

GEORGE BERNARD SHAW

GOD WILL NEVER, NEVER, NEVER LET US DOWN
IF WE HAVE FAITH AND PUT OUR TRUST IN HIM.
HE WILL ALWAYS LOOK AFTER US.

MOTHER TERESA

THINK OF IT—NOT ONE WHORLED FINGER
EXACTLY LIKE ANOTHER! IF GOD SHOULD TAKE
SUCH DELIGHT IN DESIGNING FINGERTIPS,
THINK HOW MUCH PLEASURE THE UNFURLING
OF YOUR LIFE MUST GIVE HIM.

LUCIE CHRISTOPHER

"The joy of the LORD is your strength."

NEHEMIAH 8:10 NIV

They can conquer who believe they can.

RALPH WALDO EMERSON

SUCCESS IS TO BE MEASURED NOT SO MUCH BY
THE POSITION THAT ONE HAS REACHED IN LIFE
AS BY THE OBSTACLES WHICH HE HAS
OVERCOME TRYING TO SUCCEED.

BOOKER T. WASHINGTON

EVERY PERSON YOU MEET KNOWS SOMETHING
YOU DON'T. LEARN FROM THEM.

H. JACKSON BROWN JR.

It is not enough to have a good mind;
the main thing is to use it well.

RENÉ DESCARTES

USE WHAT TALENTS YOU POSSESS;
THE WOODS WOULD BE VERY SILENT IF NO
BIRDS SANG EXCEPT THOSE THAT SANG BEST.

HENRY VAN DYKE

YOU CANNOT DISCOVER NEW OCEANS
UNLESS YOU HAVE THE COURAGE TO
LOSE SIGHT OF THE SHORE.

UNKNOWN

DID YOU EVER SEE AN UNHAPPY HORSE?
DID YOU EVER SEE A BIRD THAT HAD THE BLUES?
ONE REASON WHY BIRDS AND HORSES ARE
NOT UNHAPPY IS BECAUSE THEY ARE NOT TRYING
TO IMPRESS OTHER BIRDS AND HORSES.

DALE CARNEGIE

In everything you do, put God first,
and he will direct you and crown
your efforts with success.

PROVERBS 3:6 TLB

What you achieve through the journey of life is not as important as who you become.

UNKNOWN

WHEN ONE DOOR CLOSES, ANOTHER ONE OPENS;
BUT WE OFTEN LOOK SO LONG AND REGRETFULLY
AT THE CLOSED DOOR THAT WE FAIL TO SEE
THE ONE THAT HAS OPENED FOR US.

ALEXANDER GRAHAM BELL

CHANGE IS THE LAW OF LIFE.
AND THOSE WHO LOOK ONLY TO THE PAST
OR PRESENT ARE CERTAIN TO MISS THE FUTURE.

JOHN F. KENNEDY

A successful person is a dreamer whom someone believed in.

UNKNOWN

GO CONFIDENTLY IN THE
DIRECTION OF YOUR DREAMS.
LIVE THE LIFE YOU'VE IMAGINED.

HENRY DAVID THOREAU

The best thing about the future
is that it comes one day at a time.

ABRAHAM LINCOLN

You gain strength, courage, and confidence by every experience in which you really stop to look fear in the face. You must do the thing that you think you cannot do.

Eleanor Roosevelt

"BE STRONG AND OF GOOD COURAGE,
DO NOT FEAR NOR BE AFRAID. . .
FOR THE LORD YOUR GOD. . .
WILL NOT LEAVE YOU NOR FORSAKE YOU."

DEUTERONOMY 31:6 NKJV

We aim above the mark
to hit the mark.

RALPH WALDO EMERSON

Every tomorrow has two handles.
We can take hold of it with the handle
of anxiety or the handle of faith.

Henry Ward Beecher

Twenty years from now you will be more disappointed by the things that you didn't do than by the ones you did do. So throw off the bowlines. Sail away from the safe harbor. Catch the trade winds in your sails. Explore. Dream. Discover.

Mark Twain

ALWAYS DREAM AND SHOOT HIGHER THAN YOU KNOW HOW TO. DON'T BOTHER JUST TO BE BETTER THAN YOUR CONTEMPORARIES OR PREDECESSORS. TRY TO BE BETTER THAN YOURSELF.

WILLIAM FAULKNER

There is nothing like a dream
to create the future.

VICTOR HUGO

IF YOU HAVE BUILT CASTLES IN THE AIR,
YOUR WORK NEED NOT BE LOST;
THAT IS WHERE THEY SHOULD BE.
NOW PUT THE FOUNDATIONS UNDER THEM.

HENRY DAVID THOREAU

With men it is impossible, but not with God:
for with God all things are possible.

MARK 10:27 KJV

GREAT BEAUTY, GREAT STRENGTH, AND
GREAT RICHES ARE REALLY AND TRULY OF
NO GREAT USE; A RIGHT HEART EXCEEDS ALL.

BENJAMIN FRANKLIN

HAPPINESS WILL NEVER COME TO THOSE WHO FAIL
TO APPRECIATE WHAT THEY ALREADY HAVE.

UNKNOWN

It is easier to do a job right than to explain why you didn't.

Martin Van Buren

Great people are those who
can make others feel that they,
too, can become great.

MARK TWAIN

A PESSIMIST SEES THE DIFFICULTY IN
EVERY OPPORTUNITY; AN OPTIMIST SEES
THE OPPORTUNITY IN EVERY DIFFICULTY.

WINSTON CHURCHILL

DO NOT ASK THE LORD TO GUIDE
YOUR FOOTSTEPS IF YOU ARE NOT
WILLING TO MOVE YOUR FEET.

UNKNOWN

I can do all things through
Christ who strengthens me.

PHILIPPIANS 4:13 NKJV

REFLECT UPON YOUR PRESENT BLESSINGS,
OF WHICH EVERY MAN HAS MANY—
NOT ON YOUR PAST MISFORTUNES,
OF WHICH ALL MEN HAVE SOME.

CHARLES DICKENS

Many an opportunity is lost
because a man is out looking
for four-leaf clovers.

Anonymous

CHARACTER MAY BE MANIFESTED IN
THE GREAT MOMENTS, BUT IT IS
MADE IN THE SMALL ONES.

PHILLIPS BROOKS

Always do right; this will gratify
some people and astonish the rest.

MARK TWAIN

Keep your face to the sunshine
and you cannot see the shadow.

HELEN KELLER

DO NOT GO WHERE THE PATH MAY LEAD;
GO INSTEAD WHERE THERE IS NO
PATH AND LEAVE A TRAIL.

RALPH WALDO EMERSON

Trust in the Lord with all thine heart;
and lean not unto thine own understanding.
In all thy ways acknowledge him,
and he shall direct thy paths.

Proverbs 3:5-6 KJV

Right is right, even if everyone is against it; and wrong is wrong, even if everyone is for it.

William Penn

ASSOCIATE YOURSELF WITH MEN
OF GOOD QUALITY IF YOU ESTEEM YOUR
OWN REPUTATION; FOR IT IS BETTER TO BE
ALONE THAN IN BAD COMPANY.

GEORGE WASHINGTON

Be nice to people on your way up,
because you'll meet them
on your way down.

WILSON MIZNER

EVERY TIME YOU MAKE A CHOICE YOU ARE
TURNING THE CENTRAL PART OF YOU, THE PART
THAT CHOOSES, INTO SOMETHING A LITTLE
DIFFERENT THAN WHAT IT WAS BEFORE.

C. S. LEWIS

One falsehood spoils a thousand truths.

AFRICAN PROVERB

Everything that is done in
this world is done by hope.

MARTIN LUTHER

IF YOU EVER FIND HAPPINESS BY HUNTING FOR IT,
YOU WILL FIND IT AS THE OLD WOMAN DID HER LOST
SPECTACLES, SAFE ON HER OWN NOSE ALL THE TIME.

JOSH BILLINGS

"LOVE THE LORD YOUR GOD WITH ALL YOUR HEART AND WITH ALL YOUR SOUL AND WITH ALL YOUR STRENGTH AND WITH ALL YOUR MIND."

LUKE 10:27 NIV

More things are wrought by prayer
than this world dreams of.

ALFRED, LORD TENNYSON

NOTHING HURTS SO MUCH AS DISSATISFACTION WITH OUR CIRCUMSTANCES. . . . GOD KNOWS WHAT HE IS DOING, AND THERE IS NOTHING ACCIDENTAL IN THE LIFE OF THE BELIEVER. NOTHING BUT GOOD CAN COME TO THOSE WHO ARE WHOLLY HIS.

WATCHMAN NEE

Try not to become a success,
but rather try to become
a person of value.

ALBERT EINSTEIN

The time is always right to do what is right.

MARTIN LUTHER KING JR.

NOTHING GREAT WAS EVER
ACHIEVED WITHOUT ENTHUSIASM.

RALPH WALDO EMERSON

BE PATIENT WITH EVERYONE,
BUT ABOVE ALL WITH THYSELF. I MEAN,
DO NOT BE DISHEARTENED BY YOUR IMPERFECTIONS,
BUT ALWAYS RISE UP WITH FRESH COURAGE.

FRANCIS DE SALES

"So in everything, do to others what you would have them do to you."

MATTHEW 7:12 NIV

It is not only prayer that gives
God glory but work.

Gerard Manley Hopkins

The wisest mind has something yet to learn.

GEORGE SANTAYANA

Too much and too little
education hinder the mind.

BLAISE PASCAL

IF ONE ADVANCES CONFIDENTLY IN THE DIRECTION OF HIS DREAMS AND ENDEAVORS TO LIVE THE LIFE WHICH HE HAS IMAGINED, HE WILL MEET WITH SUCCESS UNEXPECTED IN COMMON HOURS.

HENRY DAVID THOREAU

REPUTATION IS WHAT MEN AND WOMEN
THINK OF US; CHARACTER IS WHAT GOD
AND ANGELS KNOW OF US.

THOMAS PAINE

The man who removes a mountain begins
by carrying away small stones.

CHINESE PROVERB

Whoever loves discipline loves knowledge,
but he who hates correction is stupid.

PROVERBS 12:1 NIV

THE NOBLEST QUESTION IN THE WORLD IS,
"WHAT GOOD MAY I DO IN IT?"

BENJAMIN FRANKLIN

Vision is the art of seeing things invisible.

JONATHAN SWIFT

KEEP YOUR FEET ON THE GROUND, BUT LET YOUR
HEART SOAR AS HIGH AS IT WILL. REFUSE TO BE
AVERAGE OR TO SURRENDER TO THE CHILL
OF YOUR SPIRITUAL ENVIRONMENT.

A. W. TOZER

THE SECRET TO SUCCESS IS TO DO
THE COMMON THINGS UNCOMMONLY WELL.

JOHN D. ROCKEFELLER JR.

By perseverance,
the snail reached the ark.

CHARLES H. SPURGEON

Make your work to be in
keeping with your purpose.

LEONARDO DA VINCI

All things are possible to him who believes, more to him who hopes, even more to him who loves, and more still to him who practices and perseveres in these three virtues.

Brother Lawrence

"But as for you, be strong and do not give up, for your work will be rewarded."

2 CHRONICLES 15:7 NIV

MAKE THE LEAST ADO ABOUT YOUR
GREATEST GIFTS. BE CONTENT TO ACT,
AND LEAVE THE TALKING TO OTHERS.

BALTASAR GRACIÁN

GOOD CHARACTER. . .IS NOT GIVEN TO US.
WE HAVE TO BUILD IT PIECE BY PIECE—
BY THOUGHT, CHOICE, COURAGE,
AND DETERMINATION.

H. JACKSON BROWN JR.

Act quickly; think slowly.

GREEK PROVERB

IF A GREAT THING CAN BE DONE AT ALL,
IT CAN BE DONE EASILY. BUT IT IS THE KIND OF
EASE WITH WHICH A TREE BLOSSOMS AFTER
LONG YEARS OF GATHERING STRENGTH.

JOHN RUSKIN

CONDITIONS ARE NEVER JUST RIGHT.
PEOPLE WHO DELAY ACTION UNTIL ALL FACTORS
ARE FAVORABLE ARE THE KIND WHO DO NOTHING.

WILLIAM FEATHER

Faith consists in believing when it is beyond the power of reason to believe.

Voltaire

"IF YOU HAVE FAITH AS SMALL AS A MUSTARD
SEED, YOU CAN SAY TO THIS MOUNTAIN,
'MOVE FROM HERE TO THERE' AND IT WILL MOVE.
NOTHING WILL BE IMPOSSIBLE FOR YOU."

MATTHEW 17:20-21 NIV

THE ULTIMATE CAN ONLY BE EXPRESSED
IN CONDUCT. EXAMPLE MOVES THE WORLD
MORE THAN DOCTRINE.

HENRY MILLER

Laziness means more
work in the long run.

C. S. LEWIS

To change and to improve
are two different things.

GERMAN PROVERB

LET HIM THAT WOULD MOVE
THE WORLD FIRST MOVE HIMSELF.

SOCRATES

Live to shed joys on others.
Thus best shall your own
happiness be secured.

HENRY WARD BEECHER

It is God to whom and with whom we travel,
and while He is the End of our journey,
He is also at every stopping place.

Elisabeth Elliot

The Word of God is...
an infallible guiding light for hearts.

OWEN FORD FAULKENBERRY

"IF YOU BELIEVE, YOU WILL RECEIVE
WHATEVER YOU ASK FOR IN PRAYER."

MATTHEW 21:22 NIV

IF A MAN DOES NOT KEEP PACE WITH HIS COMPANIONS, PERHAPS IT IS BECAUSE HE HEARS A DIFFERENT DRUMMER. LET HIM STEP TO THE MUSIC HE HEARS, HOWEVER MEASURED OR FAR AWAY.

HENRY DAVID THOREAU

KEEP A CLEAR EYE TOWARD LIFE'S END.
DO NOT FORGET YOUR PURPOSE AND DESTINY
AS GOD'S CREATURE. WHAT YOU ARE IN HIS SIGHT
IS WHAT YOU ARE AND NOTHING MORE.

FRANCIS OF ASSISI

One man with belief is equal to
a thousand with only interests.

JOHN STUART MILL

LET US BELIEVE THAT GOD IS IN ALL
OUR SIMPLE DEEDS AND LEARN
TO FIND HIM THERE.

A. W. TOZER

Belief is truth held in the mind;
faith is a fire in the heart.

Joseph Fort Newton

FAITH EXPECTS FROM GOD WHAT IS
BEYOND ALL EXPECTATION.

ANDREW MURRAY

There is no exception to God's commandment to love everybody.

HENRY BUCKLEW

FINISH EACH DAY AND BE DONE WITH IT. . . .
TOMORROW IS A NEW DAY; YOU SHALL BEGIN IT
SERENELY AND WITH TOO HIGH A SPIRIT TO BE
ENCUMBERED WITH YOUR OLD NONSENSE.

RALPH WALDO EMERSON

To every thing there is a season,
and a time to every purpose under the heaven.

ECCLESIASTES 3:1 KJV

Always give people a little more love
and kindness than they deserve.

Unknown

Joy is the net of love by
which you can catch souls.

MOTHER TERESA

HAPPINESS IS AS A BUTTERFLY, WHICH, WHEN
PURSUED, IS ALWAYS JUST BEYOND OUR GRASP,
BUT WHICH, IF YOU WILL SIT DOWN QUIETLY,
MAY ALIGHT UPON YOU.

NATHANIEL HAWTHORNE

EVERY EXPERIENCE GOD GIVES US,
EVERY PERSON HE PUTS IN OUR LIVES, IS THE
PERFECT PREPARATION FOR THE FUTURE
THAT ONLY HE CAN SEE.

CORRIE TEN BOOM

THERE IS NO DUTY WE SO MUCH UNDERRATE
AS THE DUTY OF BEING HAPPY. BY BEING HAPPY
WE SOW ANONYMOUS BENEFITS UPON THE WORLD.

ROBERT LOUIS STEVENSON

KEEP YOUR FACE UPTURNED TO {GOD}
AS THE FLOWERS DO THE SUN.
LOOK, AND YOUR SOUL SHALL LIVE AND GROW.

HANNAH WHITALL SMITH

This is the day the Lord has made;
let us rejoice and be glad in it.

PSALM 118:24 NIV

FILL UP THE CREVICES OF TIME WITH
THE THINGS THAT MATTER MOST.

AMY CARMICHAEL

There are better things ahead
than any we leave behind.

C. S. Lewis

If a man is called a street sweeper, he should sweep streets even as Michelangelo painted, or Beethoven composed music, or Shakespeare wrote poetry. He should sweep streets so well that all the hosts of heaven and earth will pause to say, "Here lived a great street sweeper who did his job well."

Martin Luther King Jr.

No matter how dark things seem to be
or actually are, raise your sights and
see possibilities—always see them,
for they're always there.

Norman Vincent Peale

It is no use to grumble and complain;
It's just as cheap and easy to rejoice;
When God sorts out the weather and
sends rain—why, rain's my choice.

James Whitcomb Riley

It takes courage to grow up
and become who you really are.

E. E. CUMMINGS

GOD CREATED YOU. HE KNOWS YOU AND EVERY ASPECT OF YOU. HIS LOVE FOR YOU IS BOUNDLESS, AND HIS JOY IN YOU COMES FULL CIRCLE EACH TIME YOU CALL HIM INTO YOUR LIFE IN PRAYER.

KAREN MOORE

Rejoice evermore. Pray without ceasing. In every thing give thanks.

1 THESSALONIANS 5:16-18 KJV

Always be a first-rate version of yourself,
instead of a second-rate version
of somebody else.

JUDY GARLAND

God, grant me the serenity to accept the things I cannot change, the courage to change the things I can, and the wisdom to know the difference.

Reinhold Niebuhr

If you would attain to what you are not yet,
you must always be displeased by what you are.
For where you are pleased with yourself,
there you have remained. Keep adding,
keep walking, and keep advancing.

Augustine

Our capacity to choose changes constantly with our practice of life. The longer we continue to make the wrong decisions, the more our heart hardens; the more often we make the right decisions, the more our heart softens or better, perhaps, comes alive.

Erich Fromm

ART IS A COLLABORATION BETWEEN GOD
AND THE ARTIST, AND THE LESS THE
ARTIST DOES THE BETTER.

ANDRÉ GIDE

Faith is taking the first step even
when you don't see the whole staircase.

Martin Luther King Jr.

WE MAKE A LIVING BY WHAT WE GET;
WE MAKE A LIFE BY WHAT WE GIVE.

WINSTON CHURCHILL

Courage is fear that has said its prayers.

Dorothy Bernard

SPEND TIME EACH DAY CONVERSING WITH GOD. . .
AND ASK HIM FOR THE STRENGTH AND FAITH
YOU NEED TO MEET YOUR FAILURES
AND YOUR SUCCESSES HEAD-ON.

KELLY WILLIAMS

Moments will come in your life when reason will utterly fail you. Your joy will be full as you realize that faith is your anchor, your stronghold in any storm, and your light in the deepest shadows of doubt.

Karen Moore

He who counts the stars and calls them by their names is in no danger of forgetting His own children. He knows your case as thoroughly as if you were the only creature He ever made, or the only saint He ever loved.

CHARLES H. SPURGEON

Every evening I turn my worries over to God.
He's going to be up all night anyway.

Mary C. Crowley

YOUR WORST DAYS ARE NEVER SO BAD THAT YOU
ARE BEYOND THE REACH OF GOD'S GRACE.
AND YOUR BEST DAYS ARE NEVER SO GOOD
THAT YOU ARE BEYOND THE NEED FOR GOD'S GRACE.

UNKNOWN

The mother eagle teaches her little ones to fly by making their nest so uncomfortable that they are forced to leave it and commit themselves to the unknown world of air outside. And just so does our God to us.

Hannah Whitall Smith

I NEVER HAD A POLICY;
I HAVE JUST TRIED TO DO MY
VERY BEST EACH AND EVERY DAY.

ABRAHAM LINCOLN

"Love your enemies and pray
for those who persecute you."

Matthew 5:44 niv

If there is any kindness I can show,
or any good thing I can do to any
fellow being, let me do it now,
and not deter or neglect it,
as I shall not pass this way again.

William Penn

Spread love everywhere you go. . . .
Let no one ever come to you without
leaving better and happier.

MOTHER TERESA

'TIS A LESSON YOU SHOULD HEED:
TRY, TRY AGAIN.
IF AT FIRST YOU DON'T SUCCEED,
TRY, TRY AGAIN.

W. E. HICKSON

THE VERY BEST AND HIGHEST ATTAINMENT
IN THIS LIFE IS TO REMAIN STILL AND LET
GOD ACT AND SPEAK IN YOU.

MEISTER ECKHART

Everyone you meet is fighting some kind of battle, and your smile, your kind word, your hand of friendship will make a difference in their day and will change how they see things. You can be the change. You can bless those around you.

Karen Moore

THERE ARE TWO WAYS OF SPREADING LIGHT:
TO BE THE CANDLE OR THE
MIRROR THAT REFLECTS IT.

EDITH WHARTON

"Man looks at the outward appearance,
but the Lord looks at the heart."

1 Samuel 16:7 niv

GOD WRITES THE GOSPEL NOT IN
THE BIBLE ALONE, BUT ON TREES AND FLOWERS
AND CLOUDS AND STARS.

MARTIN LUTHER

Patience serves as a protection against wrongs as clothes do against cold.

LEONARDO DA VINCI

PRAYER ENLARGES THE HEART UNTIL IT IS
CAPABLE OF CONTAINING GOD'S GIFT OF HIMSELF.
ASK AND SEEK AND YOUR HEART WILL GROW
BIG ENOUGH TO RECEIVE HIM.

MOTHER TERESA

TODAY, WELL LIVED, MAKES EVERY
YESTERDAY A DREAM OF HAPPINESS
AND EVERY TOMORROW A VISION OF HOPE.

SANSKRIT PROVERB

Great works are performed not by strength but by perseverance.

SAMUEL JOHNSON

One sees great things from the valley;
only small things from the peak.

G. K. CHESTERTON

I AM AN OLD MAN AND HAVE KNOWN
A GREAT MANY TROUBLES, BUT MOST OF THEM
HAVE NEVER HAPPENED.

MARK TWAIN

EACH OF YOU SHOULD LOOK NOT ONLY TO YOUR OWN INTERESTS, BUT ALSO TO THE INTERESTS OF OTHERS. YOUR ATTITUDE SHOULD BE THE SAME AS THAT OF CHRIST JESUS.

PHILIPPIANS 2:4-5 NIV

To know even one life has breathed
easier because you have lived. . .
this is to have succeeded.

RALPH WALDO EMERSON

MANY THINGS WILL HAPPEN IN YOUR LIFE THAT YOU CANNOT CHANGE. MOST WILL NOT BE IN YOUR CONTROL. WISDOM COMES FROM LEARNING TO KEEP YOUR EYES ON THE ONE WHO IS IN CONTROL.

KAREN MOORE

Earth has no sorrow that Heaven cannot heal.

THOMAS MORE

YOU CAN KEEP A FAITH ONLY AS YOU CAN KEEP
A PLANT, BY ROOTING IT INTO YOUR LIFE
AND MAKING IT GROW THERE.

PHILLIPS BROOKS

A FORGIVENESS OUGHT TO BE LIKE A CANCELED NOTE, TORN IN TWO AND BURNED UP, SO THAT IT CAN NEVER BE SHOWN AGAINST THE MAN.

HENRY WARD BEECHER

The future is full of doubt,
indeed, but fuller still of hope.

JOHN LUBBOCK

THAT WHICH EACH CAN DO BEST,
NONE BUT HIS MAKER CAN TEACH HIM.

RALPH WALDO EMERSON

"SEEK FIRST THE KINGDOM OF GOD AND HIS RIGHTEOUSNESS, AND ALL THESE THINGS SHALL BE ADDED TO YOU."

MATTHEW 6:33 NKJV

YOUR FATHER WILL HOLD YOU IN HIS HAND
AND SHAPE YOU ACCORDING TO HIS WILL AND
PURPOSE AS LONG AS YOU ARE WILLING TO LET HIM.

KAREN MOORE

Where our work is, there let our joy be.

TERTULLIAN

DEVELOP SUCCESS FROM FAILURES.
DISCOURAGEMENT AND FAILURE ARE TWO OF
THE SUREST STEPPING-STONES TO SUCCESS.

DALE CARNEGIE

LOVE IS THE GREATEST THING THAT GOD CAN GIVE US; FOR HE HIMSELF IS LOVE; AND IT IS THE GREATEST THING WE CAN GIVE TO GOD.

JEREMY TAYLOR

{GOD'S} MERCY HATH NO RELATION TO TIME,
NO LIMITATION IN TIME; IT IS NOT FIRST,
NOR LAST, BUT ETERNAL, EVERLASTING.

JOHN DONNE

ALL THE WISDOM OF THE WORLD IS CHILDISH FOOLISHNESS IN COMPARISON WITH THE ACKNOWLEDGMENT OF JESUS CHRIST.

MARTIN LUTHER

Other books were given for our information; the Bible was given for our transformation.

ANONYMOUS

You have to accept whatever comes,
and the only important thing is that
you meet it with courage and with
the best you have to give.

Eleanor Roosevelt

Laziness may appear attractive,
but work gives satisfaction.

ANNE FRANK

Genius is divine perseverance.

WOODROW WILSON

Observe people who are good at their work—
skilled workers are always in demand and
admired; they don't take a back seat to anyone.

Proverbs 22:29 MSG

REMEMBER, YOU JUST HAVE ONE REAL GOAL
AND THAT IS TO DO A WORK THAT IS PLEASING
TO THE LORD. HE WILL GO BEFORE YOU TO LEAD THE
WAY, BESIDE YOU TO COMFORT YOU ON THE JOURNEY,
AND BEHIND YOU TO PROTECT YOUR WELL-BEING.

KAREN MOORE

INSTEAD OF ALWAYS HARPING ON A MAN'S FAULTS,
TELL HIM OF HIS VIRTUES.
TRY TO PULL HIM OUT OF HIS RUT OF BAD HABITS.

ELEANOR H. PORTER

GOD'S DESIGNS REGARDING YOU,
AND HIS METHODS OF BRINGING ABOUT
THESE DESIGNS, ARE INFINITELY WISE.

MADAME GUYON

It's not how much we give but how much love we put into the giving.

MOTHER TERESA

He who labors as he prays lifts his heart to God with his hands.

BERNARD OF CLAIRVAUX

THE FUTURE IS SOMETHING WHICH EVERYONE
REACHES AT THE RATE OF SIXTY MINUTES AN
HOUR, WHATEVER HE DOES, WHOEVER HE IS.

C. S. LEWIS

Simple gratitude helps us experience God
at work in every moment of every day.

HARRIET CROSBY

OPTIMISM IS THE FAITH THAT LEADS TO ACHIEVEMENT. NOTHING CAN BE DONE WITHOUT HOPE AND CONFIDENCE.

HELEN KELLER

WHATEVER YOU DO, WORK AT IT WITH ALL YOUR HEART, AS WORKING FOR THE LORD, NOT FOR MEN.

COLOSSIANS 3:23 NIV

If you judge people,
you have no time to love them.

MOTHER TERESA

You may have to fight a battle
more than once to win it.

MARGARET THATCHER

SPEAKING BEAUTIFULLY IS LITTLE TO THE PURPOSE
UNLESS ONE LIVES BEAUTIFULLY.

ELIZABETH PRENTISS

Yearn to understand first and to be understood second.

BECA LEWIS ALLEN

LEARNING IS NOT ATTAINED BY CHANCE;
IT MUST BE SOUGHT FOR WITH ARDOR AND
ATTENDED TO WITH DILIGENCE.

ABIGAIL ADAMS

TRUE SILENCE IS THE REST OF THE MIND;
it is to the spirit what sleep is to the body,
nourishment and refreshment.

WILLIAM PENN

If you are patient in one moment of anger,
you will avoid a hundred days of sorrow.

TIBETAN PROVERB

How you respond to the events of your life is as important, if not more so, than the events themselves.

Karen Moore

LET NO MAN DESPISE THY YOUTH;
BUT BE THOU AN EXAMPLE OF THE BELIEVERS,
IN WORD, IN CONVERSATION, IN CHARITY,
IN SPIRIT, IN FAITH, IN PURITY.

1 TIMOTHY 4:12 KJV

Life is what we make it.
Always has been, always will be.

GRANDMA MOSES

Never be afraid to trust an unknown
future to a known God.

Corrie ten Boom

The future is as bright
as the promises of God.

WILLIAM CAREY

Lives of great men all remind us
we can make our lives sublime,
and departing, leave behind us
footprints on the sands of time.

Henry Wadsworth Longfellow